SIMPLE MACHINES

WOW!

Troll Associates

SIMPLE MACHINES

by Rae Bains

Illustrated by Joseph Veno

Troll Associates

Library of Congress Cataloging in Publication Data

Bains, Rae.
   Simple machines.

   Summary: Text and illustrations describe the six
simple machines upon which all others are based. These
include the pulley, the lever, the wheel, the inclined
plane, the wedge, and the screw.
   1. Simple machines—Juvenile literature.   [1. Simple
machines.   2. Machines]   I. Veno, Joseph, ill.
II. Title.
TJ147.B25   1984   621.8   84-2607
ISBN 0-8167-0166-0 (lib. bdg.)
ISBN 0-8167-0167-9 (pbk.)

The first humans lived very simple lives. They had only their hands, feet, and teeth to do work with. They lifted and carried objects with their hands. They moved other objects with their hands and feet. And they cut things like food by biting with their teeth. But humans, unlike all other animals, were able to create machines to make their work easier and faster.

The first machines were simple ones. Yet even though they did only simple jobs, they made life much better for people. And as they were improved and put to many different uses, these simple machines played a great part in the advance of civilization.

All of today's complicated machines are based on six simple machines used long ago. These six machines are the lever, the wheel, the pulley, the inclined plane, the wedge, and the screw.

The value of these machines is the mechanical advantage they give us. That means the machines help us to do a great deal of work with less effort. For example, you have probably seen a person replace a flat automobile tire with a good one. To do this, the automobile first had to be lifted.

But one person cannot lift a car without using a machine. So that person used a machine called a jack. The mechanical advantage of the jack enabled the driver to lift the heavy car up using very little effort. Every one of the six simple machines can give us some mechanical advantage.

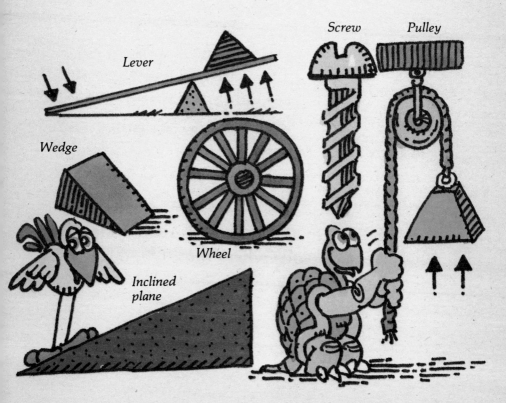

Lever

Screw

Pulley

Wedge

Wheel

Inclined plane

The first simple machine was the lever. It was probably discovered this way: Somebody wanted to move a big rock or another heavy object. When pushing by hand didn't move it, the person may have put one end of a stick between the rock and the ground, then pressed down on the other end of the stick. When the rock moved, our early ancestors had discovered the lever.

The idea of the lever is based on three things: effort, or force; distance; and balance. A lever's balance point is called its fulcrum. Every lever has a fulcrum. The fulcrum is the part of the machine that does not move. When our rock-moving ancestor pushed down on the stick, the ends of the stick moved, and the rock moved. But the fulcrum—the place where the stick balanced on the ground—did not move.

The greater the distance between the effort and the fulcrum, the greater the load is that can be moved. Suppose you want to move a rock. And suppose you can choose between a long stick and a short stick to use as a lever. The long stick will allow you to move the rock with less effort. So we say that the longer the lever, the greater its mechanical advantage will be.

A lever such as the rock-mover or a crowbar is called a first-class lever. A first-class lever has the fulcrum in the middle—between the load and the effort.

If you put the load in the middle—between the effort and the fulcrum—you have a second-class lever. A wheelbarrow is a kind of second-class lever. The wheel on the ground is the fulcrum. The load is in the barrow in the middle. And you apply the effort at the other end.

In a third-class lever, the effort is in the middle—between the load and the fulcrum. Did you ever see a picture of a castle with a drawbridge that could be pulled up to keep enemies from entering? That kind of draw-bridge is an example of a third-class lever. The fulcrum is at one end, where the bridge is fastened to the castle by a hinge. The load is at the other end. And the chains that draw the bridge up are the effort—applied in the middle, between the load and the fulcrum.

Third-class lever

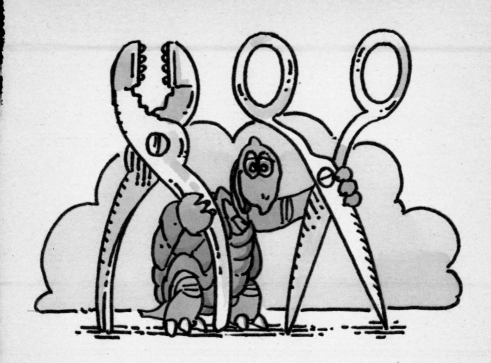

Two levers joined together—called double levers—can be used to do a job one lever cannot do. Scissors and pliers are examples of double levers. Each half of the scissors is a lever. The place where they are joined together is the fulcrum. The handles of the scissors move apart and together. The blades also move. But just as with a single lever, the scissors' fulcrum does not move. The same principle applies to other double levers, such as pliers and nutcrackers.

The next important simple machine was the wheel. With its invention, civilization took a huge leap forward. Using two wheels, connected by a rod or stick called an axle, people long ago made chariots and carts. With four wheels and two axles, they made wagons.

A wheel turned on its side became the basis for a number of different machines. There was the grindstone, or grinding wheel, that turned grain into flour, and the potter's wheel for making bowls and jugs. A windmill was a wheel turned by the wind. And a water wheel was a wheel turned by rushing water.

Windmills and water wheels could be connected to a grindstone that ground grain. This made a machine that didn't need to be powered by a person or an animal.

Today, wheels are used in thousands of ways. You can see the wheels on cars, trains, bicycles, roller skates, and lawn mowers. Then there are all the things that work on the idea of the wheel, such as the gears in watches and clocks, in engines for trains, planes, and sewing machines. Our lives would be very different without the wheel!

Another basic machine is the pulley. A simple pulley uses a wheel and a rope. The wheel provides a round, grooved track for the rope to run through. With a simple pulley, an effort can be applied in one direction, and a load can be moved in another direction.

At the top of a sailboat's mast there is a single fixed pulley for raising and lowering a sail. It is much easier to pull down than to pull up a load. That is because when you pull down, the weight of your own body can be used.

If you combine one fixed pulley and one movable pulley in a system known as a block and tackle, you can do twice as much work with the same effort.

The hoists used to lift heavy weights for building construction are double or triple pulleys. Pulleys also lift the scaffolds for sign painters and window cleaners. They may have very high mechanical advantages.

The inclined plane is another simple machine that makes work easier. A slope, such as the side of a hill, is a natural inclined plane. A ramp, or the slanted gangplank of a ship, is an inclined plane made by people.

Have you ever watched furniture movers loading a truck? They put a heavy piece of furniture onto a wheeled board and pull or push it up a ramp that goes from the ground into the truck. It would be extremely difficult for the movers to lift a large piano or refrigerator in their arms. But the inclined plane makes it a job that can be done quickly, safely, and with far less effort.

An inclined plane stays in place while it is being used. The wedge, which has a slanted shape like an inclined plane, is a simple machine that works by being moved. A wedge is pointed at one end and wider at the other end. An axe blade is a wedge, and so are a knife blade, the point of a nail, and a sewing needle.

The point of a wedge makes an opening, then the rest of the wedge is driven in. Imagine trying to hammer a nail without a point or split a log with a round-edged axe, and you'll understand what a valuable machine the wedge is.

In addition to the wedge, there is another simple machine based on the idea of the inclined plane. It is the screw. The screw is really an inclined plane that goes around and around.

If you look at a screw, you'll see that the groove has the same kind of slope as an inclined plane. The major difference is that the screw spirals as it goes from the tip toward the head of the screw.

Screws hold things together much better than nails do. You can't pull a screw out of a piece of wood as easily as you can pull out a nail. That's because the threads, or spiral, of

the screw have a much stronger grip than the nail.

We use screws to do many jobs. Almost all of our complicated machines are put together with dozens of screws. The bases of most light bulbs are screws. And some water pumps work by pushing water along the grooves of a big screw.

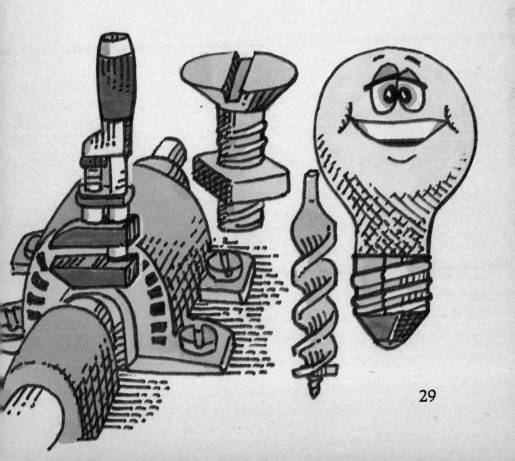

To most people, the word *machine* means a huge, complicated device run by motors. But these huge devices are really many, little simple machines all working together. At home, in school, outside, just about anywhere imaginable, you can see the six basic machines at work. From eggbeaters to screw-top jars, from record players to tape recorders, from spaceships to submarines, if you look closely, you will see the six simple machines—the lever, the wheel, the pulley, the inclined plane, the wedge, and the screw.